The Beauty
Family Poetry

This book is dedicated to my beautiful family.

Introduction

Gary has spent many years perfecting his writing style.
He hopes to attract a variety of readers of all ages and
backgrounds with his belief that poetry should be
inclusive, diverse, virtuous and heartwarming.

In this book you will find something for all the family.

This is Gary's second book. His first anthology titled
'The Wandering Lyricist' was published by Augur Press
back in July 2019 (available online worldwide).

Gary lives in Nottingham with his wife and two children.

Follow him on Twitter @PoetNottingham

List of Contents

Visit England

We love living in England
Even when it starts to rain
Because we say we're used to it
And exclaim, "here it is again!"
We grab our coats and hat
Slip on our sensible shoes
Make ready with our umbrella
After the weather forecast on the news
Dash out into the downpour
Splash through deepening puddles
Have a battle with the high winds
Under our umbrella, in a huddle

Therefore. visit us in England
You could hop onto the next plane
For sunbathing must bore you
Come, experience first-class rain!

Street Poetry

Standing in the street
I love to chat
Delivering rhymes to people
In my shirt and peak cap
If they stop and listen
I have tales to tell
About faraway places
Situations and feelings as well
Then they go on their way
When we are through
Occasionally thoughtful
And hopefully entertained too
For this is my passion
Reciting straight from the heart
Writing is my life
Street poetry is my art

Moonlit Romance

Light from the stars
Glowing in the night
Twinkling and shimmering
A beautiful white
On a black satin backdrop
They sparkle so bright
We look upwards together
Through the old skylight
Completely in awe
At the beauty of the night
Our arms entwined
Holding each other tight
We feel one another's warmth
Below the old skylight
Finding the stars so pretty
The clock chimes midnight

Red Roses

A bunch of red roses
Standing in a vase
Ten to be precise
On a sideboard near the stairs

Looking bright and healthy
With water nice and clear
Supported by straight stems
Their fragrance fills the air

Ten red roses
Our picture hangs above
Picturing our wedding day
Me and you, looking in love

Green leaves looking vibrant
Petals soft and fresh
Thorns have been removed
Together, we are blessed

Beach Holiday - Aspiration

Take us to where the air is fresh
To a beach where palm trees sway
Where gentle waves lap the shore
That's where we want to spend our day

Let us lie down on stripy sun loungers
Under umbrellas with cocktails too
Wearing our sunshades and our bathers
Looking out into the purest blue

We'd enjoy the salty sea air
Watch our children playing in the sand
Building sandcastles with their buckets
Whist listening to the seaside band

We'd like to paddle along the shoreline
Maybe have a swim in the lukewarm sea
Collect sea shells and colourful pebbles
At the beach is where we want to be

Beach Holiday - Reality

Arriving at a totally packed beach
And it is starting to spot with rain
We find a space to throw out our towel
Then the kids run off, it's their game

We chase them like headless chickens
'Stay around us', we both demand
'And if you do this, we will treat you
With a trip to the ice cream stand'

Therefore, the children grumble but stay
At our feet they begin to dig around
Gently at first, then more vigorously
Pelting us both with grains of sand

After we brush the sand off our faces
We smile at our children and say
'Isn't this a relaxing day on the beach!
Just how long would you like to stay?'

Water-Blue

I have dived deeply
Into your water of blue
I swam eagerly
Down and through
I have touched the depths
At your water's floor
Before coming back for air
And down again once more
Yet after all my observations
I have failed to understand
Your water of blue
And its threshold of sand

Give me Coffee

I like my coffee in the morning
I like my coffee instead of tea
I like my coffee at lunch time
It gets me through the working day

I like coffee at my breaktime
I like my coffee when I get home
I like coffee with my dinner
Even when I'm on the telephone

I like my coffee in the evening
I like coffee for a bedtime treat
I think coffee is amazing
Until I struggle to get to sleep!

Story Time

Will you choose a book
That I can read to you?
Because it's your bedtime now
So please settle down too
Hand over your choice
As you climb into bed
I'm placing my chair adjacent
Next to you and Ted
I shall deliver the story
In a way that you can see
All the lovely illustrations
From the book on my knee
And if you're ready
I shall now read the first chapter
Once upon a time there was…
A very hungry velociraptor!

Dragon Fire

The moon shone
In the middle of the night
Over a silent castle
That came into sight
When a dragon swooped
Roaring with all of his might
'You'd better stay
Out of my way!'

The people of the castle
Laid down low
Daring not to move
The dragon would know
But their impatience
Started to grow
So, they all shouted
'Go away!'

Therefore, the beast
Came to have his feast
Breathing out fire
Baring razor sharp teeth
Flying down
Towards the courtyard beneath
Snarling, 'come here'
'I will gobble you up!'

The dragon landed
On the castle keep
But not one person
Did his wicked eyes meet
So, he stomped around
On his enormous feet
Thinking this will
Frighten them out!

But the people hid
All silent and brave
Waiting for the dragon
To return to his cave
But instead he landed
In the courtyard and gave
A ROAR!!
And spat out his flames!

Suddenly, out dashed a knight
On a fine-looking steed
With a shield and a lance
Travelling with speed
Towards an onlooking dragon
That gave out a shriek
As the knight chased it
Away into the sky!
Hurray!!!

Ava's Song

In the middle of the ocean
On an island, inside a cave
Lives a beautiful Mermaid
Blond hair woven into a braid
Ava sits upon a rock
She sings to the ocean waves
Music so enchanting
Fish seem to stop and gaze
Ava splashes her blue tail
Making the fish dart away
Only to swim a few yards
To come back straight away
And on goes her song
One of contentment and joy
About the lush green island
The white sands at its shore
Mentioning coconuts, palm trees
Crabs and iguanas
Parrots and green turtles
Mangos and bananas
Ava sings to her friends
Swimming, outside the cave
Who play, duck and dive
Amongst the gentle ocean waves

Fairy Cottage

In a former post office
Near an old railroad
Live the fairies
In their humble abode
They flutter and flitter
Sing and dance
Sprinkle fairy dust
At every given chance
However, sometimes
They must hide away
When the humans come
For their holiday stay

At night they twirl
In glistening swirls
Casting spells
Careful not to be heard
They clean the pots
And mop the floors
Iron shirts
Tidy the drawers
But the fairies know
As morning appears
Visitors will wake up
So they disappear

Matchstick Man

Draw him carefully
If you possibly can
With a Black felt tip pen
A matchstick man.
Then create a world
Where he can dwell
By painting some grass
Drawing trees as well.
Now he can walk
Run and jump
Do summersaults
Land on his rump
But wait. He needs a house!
Where he can stay?
Draw walls and windows
A roof in grey
Then a white picket fence
A gate and a door
Some flowers in his garden
For him to care for.
The matchstick man
Now seems kind of happy
But wait. No girlfriend!
Who will he marry?

A Rocket Full of Aliens

Zoom, zoom, zoom they go
Around the Milky Way
Flying past lots of planets
Trying to find somewhere to stay

One hundred billion planets
Far too many to make a choice
A no to Mercury and Venus
Earth looks way too moist

Mars is way too small and red
Jupiter, too full of gas
Saturn's ring has put them off
On Uranus they wouldn't last

Next, they stop at Neptune
Where they consider putting a dome
But they agree it's much too windy
So, the Aliens head for home

Returning back through space
Past the planets of the Milky Way
Eventually arriving at Kepler-69c
Home, where they decide to stay

Sleepy Mouse

Over the hills
And far away
Awakes a sleepy mouse
In a bale of hay.
He pops his nose out
To smell the air
The winter has gone
Time to reappear.
Peeping from the hay
He looks about
Gives a squeak of delight
Before scurrying out
Into a barn
Between snorting pigs
Through a chicken's feet
Into a pile of twigs.
The sweet scent of flowers
Fills the air
What joy he feels
Spring is finally here!

Monkey House

Deep inside the jungle
A Monkey sits in a tree
He dreams of sipping coffee
And eating scones for his tea

Bored of yellow bananas
Tired of climbing trees
His preference would be a latte
In a cup and saucer on his knee

His scone would be buttered
Then layered with strawberry jam
Comfortably sitting upon a sofa
Watching a television programme

Teaching him all about humans
And why they cut down trees
When they could rather recycle
Their paper cups, furniture and settees

Ten Soldiers

One little drummer boy
Beats on his drum
Rat-a-tat-tat
Having so much fun
Ten painted soldiers
Wearing bearskin hats
Left foot, right foot
Over the garden grass
Ten little red coats
All in a line
One, two, three, four
Marching in time
Ten little figurines
Saluting on parade
'ATTENTION!' Comes the command
'Would you like Lemonade?'

Niamh the Pixie

Niamh is four inches tall
With pointed little ears
She has a mischievous grin
And is ageless in years
She wears a pointed hat
Over her green short hair
Red and yellow wings
For flitting through the air
Her skin tone is blue
With a cute little nose
Her shoes come to a point
She wears rags for clothes
Niamh lives in a forest
Near the blue ocean sea
She has her home in a hole
In the hollow of a tree
She has dust in her pockets
For people that come too near
She'll sprinkle it over them
Into their unsuspecting hair
Then she will giggle as they float
Off the floor, into the air
So, watch out for Niamh
Or she'll catch you unawares

Niamh's Song

A little bit of sneaking
A little bit of magic
A sprinkling of pixie dust
And there you have it!
Up you go
Into the sky
Up, up, up you go
Going so very high
Oh My!!

Monster on the Landing

Daddy, did you know?

A monster lives on our landing
With green fur and bulging eyes
It grumbles when it gets hungry
I think it never, ever smiles
Its paws must be the size of shovels
Because it stomps, creaks and knocks
Clumsily waking me from my sleep
Almost always at twelve o'clock
At which time I hide under my duvet
And wait for it to walk on
I think it goes in our bathroom too
Due to a flush, click and a yawn
Then it creaks back across our landing
With those green ginormous paws
Grumbling and bumping into things
Opening and closing our doors
I've heard a monster on our landing
And it's only ever there at night
Someday I'm going to have a look
But maybe not tonight!

Christmas Eve

There is a sleepy village in Lapland
Where letters arrive every day
From children all over the world
Asking for toys to fit in Santa's sleigh

Which are delivered to his quaint little house
Beautifully decorated, red and white clad
Where Santa opens them individually
Discovering whether they've been good or bad

Then he decides on his list for the children
What toys the elves should make
On which he ponders so passionately
Whist eating his mince pies, freshly baked

With a ho, ho, ho, he chuckles
As he watches the elves' labour of love
For lunch he feeds his reindeer Rudolf
With carrots from his snuggly white glove

As Christmas Eve night arrives
He excitedly fills his sleigh to the top
With bulging red sacks full of presents
And they take off with a gallop and a hop

Up and through the clouds they soar
Then downwards to snowy white roofs
Where he lands his sleigh very gently
To pop down a sooty chimney shoot

He sneaks across the living room carpet
Leaving a generous gift under the tree
Then he consumes the mince pies and sherry
Wiping the crumbs up so no one will see

He wriggles back up the chimney
And returns to his red and white sleigh
Then it's off to the next house on the list
To prepare everyone for Christmas Day

Eric the Dog

Much loved Eric is no trouble
I'm told he's not a mischievous dog
Apparently, the only thing he does
Is sit on my friend's conservatory rug
Looking out over the garden
Without the slightest urge to bark
He never asks them to go out and play
Or go for a walk at the local park
Never makes a mess of their furnishings
Or cries when no-body's at home
Nor does he cost them a penny to keep
He's never chewed a single bone
That's because Eric isn't a real dog
This pooch was made faraway, overseas
By a Bulgarian surprisingly called Eric
Crafted with loving hands and expertise

Supremacy

Once upon a time, a long time ago
There lived a king in a castle of gold
His name was King Peter the Great
He believed he was strong, brave and bold
His banner presented a yellow laurel wreath
Below the letters printed Au
His armour was the envy of all
In the most beautiful metallic blue
His sword was solid gold
His shield was embellished with gems
The horse he rode was the finest steed
Which he jousted on against all of his friends
In a competition that was called Supremacy
In which King Peter could never lose
His friends the knights were paid by him
To fall from their horse for any excuse
The crowd would haplessly applaud the King
As he stood victorious over the knights lay slain
It was obvious to every spectator present
That bravery King Peter could never proclaim

Half a Bubble Off Plumb

Sometimes I think I'm....

A sandwich short of a picnic
Two bricks short of a load
As nutty as a fruitcake
I've switched into crazy mode!

I'm flying away with the fairies
As mad as a box of frogs
My head is full of stump water
I think I'm crazier than a fox!

I'm as loopy as a soup sandwich
I have bugs living inside my brain
I'm as mad as a mad hatter's tea party
That's totally and utterly insane!

I'm knitting with only one needle
As loony as a March hare
Even loopier than a cross-eyed cowboy
But what do I really care!

The Awakening

First flowers
Draw me toward
Colours bright
In the fresh sunshine

Yellow daffodils
Lend me your charm
In picking one
It shall be mine

Snowdrops
Innocent and white
Bring me contentment
From within

Bluebells
Nod me a greeting
Prompted
By the arrival of spring

Price's Piece

I am relaxing at Price's Piece
On a bench, my face is warmed by the sun
The wind is softly caressing my hair
Small insects make a gentle hum
I hear a horse trotting by
'Clippity-Clop' sounds on a beaten trail
Birds are singing from the treetops
Twittering to each other their daily mail
The sensation I feel is contentment
As I gaze up at the azure sky
Listening to the tree branches clattering
As the spring breeze gently floats by

Harmony

Happiness
Is a meadow stream
Banked by grass
Vibrant and green
With wild flowers
That jiggle about
In a soft breeze
Gentle throughout
Moving in
Between the trees
Shaking a melody
Amongst the leaves
Reminding us
This is nature's way
To deliver peace
And harmony

Sunrise Spectacular

The sun starts to climb
On what was once night
Above Haywood Oaks Lane
An offering of orange delight
Which radiates itself
Around a rising sun
Inflaming the morning
As the moon is outshone
Then a blue starts to form
Only slightly at first
Colouring the corners of the sky
Until the darkness has dispersed
Revealing a farm and its cattle
Through an abundance of trees
Once silhouetted
Amidst rolling ploughed fields
A gorgeous rising sun
Showering blessings upon me
Breathtaking in spectacle
Creating a lifetime's memory

Thunder Storm

Rumbles wake me from my slumber
Flashes of lightening light up my room
Rain bounces off the window pane
Then the night brings back the gloom
The sound of torrential rain fills my ears
From the darkness, a gushing sound
Then a rumble returns once more
Outside the rain pours onto the ground
I sit up and peer out of the window
Through a constant stream of rain
I see the houses suddenly light up
Which reflects onto the window pane
So I grip the curtains and pull,
Swishing them together, pulling them tight
Then I lie back and pay no more attention
To the unexpected storm in the night

Respite

Let me roam
Where trees are plentiful.
I want to breathe
The pure untainted air.
Step upon step
Through the bracken.
Pushing back branches, near.
Sweeping through
The golden-brown leaves.
Over logs
Lying, here and there.
In the woods
I want to be strolling.
Content
And without a care.

The Proverb

Money makes the world go around
However, does it make us all content?
Because money only buys us possessions
Until it's all but spent
Cash purchases material things
But what about our health?
An unpolluted environment for example
Can this be bought with wealth?
Every day fertile land is cleared
Buildings erected to fulfill our needs
But what happens when there are no more crops
Upon what else shall we feed?

Only when the last tree has been cut down
The last fish has been caught
The last stream poisoned
Only then, shall we realise that we can't eat money
Cree Indian Proverb

Angel Bay

We feel peaceful, rejuvenated, relaxed
At the inlet called Angel Bay
For the view is stunningly beautiful
Over a beach where huge boulders lay
The Headland is teaming with wildlife
And decorated with lush green grass
Grey Seals capture our attention
Dolphins and porpoises also swim past
This place is enchanting, delightful
The salty air and the rushing sea
We could sit and look out forever
With sandwiches and a flask of tea

Sorrento

I regarded those houses
Beautifully crafted.
And the bay
Consisted of bliss.
I'm reminiscing about a place
Called Sorrento.
For it stole my heart
With its allure and fizz.
In this town
I lost my appetite to travel.
As I walked
On those cobbled stone streets.
Views stunned me
From the Bay of Naples.
Mount Vesuvius
Prominently stood from the deep.
The town is historic and quaint.
And bustled
With the coming of night.
Illuminated in all its glory.
Go and see
For your own delight.

Guitarrista con Arte

Sweet sounds resound
From skilled finger tips
Running up and down the frets
In and out of bumps and dips.

Up and down the strings they go
Tapping their way on wood
Enthusiastically
While the right hand quickly plucks.

Tireless in their motion
Swift fingers pick in tune
Polished notes ring out magnificently
Beautiful acoustics fill the room.

Customers listen with interest
To the music he brings from Spain
Browsing and looking at artwork
Whilst drinking from flutes of champagne.

Local Football Derby

Fans sporting shirts and scarves
Fill the stadium for the ritual to begin
Impetuous passion results in fireworks
Each team has demanded a win.
Often called the funny old game'
With an atmosphere you could cut with a knife
Two goals stand each end of the field
Where the football is brought to life.
The crowd bursts into song
When each player takes to the hallowed turf
Jogging around before lining up
Eager to demonstrate their selection's worth.
Both managers came with expectations
Each fan came for a winning thrill
Let's hope this game lives up to the hype
Because last time they drew nil-nil.

Robin Hood's Drawers

"Marian!" Shouts Robin,
From behind a leafy bush.
"What size are these tights again?
They don't fit me like they should!"

"Are you sure", Asks Marian,
Whilst trying not to look.
"I bought the size you told me to.
Here! I wrote it in my book!"

"Yes!" yells Robin, "I'm sure!"
"They're chafing all my bits,
Furthermore, my knees look knobbly
Way too tight on me, to fit!"

"Your bits?" Asks Marian,
"Whatever do you mean?"
"My toes are all squished in!" Claims Robin,
"I think they're going green!"

"Come over here and let me look!"
Demands Marian, feeling rather cross.
"I'll have to take them back again
To Roving Crafters' Cloths."

Out steps Robin from the bush
To much laughter and applause
Robin's merry men have arrived shouting,
"We love your new tight drawers!"

Flying Fruit

No one had ever feared fruit before
Until one fateful day
When a thrower was hit by a banana
That had boomeranged back his way
It had flown around several houses
A tree, a man and his dog
Before knocking the thrower flat on his back
With a flash of yellow and a thud!
The townsfolk had a meeting that day
To discuss the perilous fruit
And they all voted to ban it
From any recreational, aerial pursuits!

Prosecco Mayhem

Shall we open the Prosecco wine?
But, why are you shaking up the bottle?
Now pressure has built inside
Meaning there is going to be a lot of trouble

Don't you dare aim it over here
Or you'll change my disposition
I'm anxious now and about to flee
For fear of a cork to my head collision

What do you mean the cork is stuck?
I'm not opening it for you now!
You've shaken the bottle up far too much
Open it on your own, somehow!

Why are you tugging at the cork?
With the bottle wedged between your legs?
When that thing flies off, we're in trouble
It'll whizz straight for our heads!

Can I ask, have you removed the foil?
Around the neck by pulling the string?
Blimey! DON'T DO IT NOW!
POP, whizz!!! Bang, PING!!!!!

Cheers!

The time we had
Together we shared
Fun and laughter
Our souls we bared.
Whilst we chatted
We drank a tipple or two
Those jokes I cracked
Along with you.
We sang a song
The words we knew,
That night we went out
And sunk a few!

Liberty

We shouldn't need to request
To be free.
But some leaders
Simply would disagree.
No shackles or bonds.
Or tied up tongues.
Will ever be
An appealing philosophy.

Our lives
Should be lived carefree.
Free from trouble, strife
And tyranny.
We could live in peace.
All wars would cease.
This is simply
How the world should be.

Writer's Lift

Lift your chin up
Be proud of who you are
Because lots of people
Think that you're a star
You've come a long way
To where you are today
Jumping through hoops
Progressing, day by day
Be happy, contented
A smile is all you need
To chase those blues away
In order to succeed

Me

In my heart
There is no room for hatred
In my mind
Only space for love
I deem my life
To be most sacred
A precious gift
From heaven above

Printed in Great Britain
by Amazon

84262873R00031